DMC

DYNAMIC MODEL OF CONSCIOUSNESS

BY

GEORGE ARTHUR LAREAU

SUFI GEORGE BOOKS
PHOENIX

DMC—Dynamic Model of Consciousness

Table of Contents

DMC—Dynamic Model of Consciousness

Dave, His Car, and His Mind

My birthday is in December, so I had turned 17 before Easter in my freshman year of college. McKendree still had many student Methodist ministers, mostly from Southern Illinois towns and most of them served several little rural churches on Sundays.

I was a novelty on campus, both as a "foreigner" from Massachusetts and as the youngest member of my class. That made me a popular guest preacher and I spent many Sundays riding the circuit with fellow student ministers.

My preaching amounted to little more than an announcement that there were also Christians in Massachusetts. I didn't know how to preach. But I liked to sing, so we sang a lot.

Now Dave, he was a popular senior, and he had only one church, quite a status symbol. His church was not a simple rural one, but a normal town church.

Two weeks before Easter, Dave came up to me and asked if I would like to share his Easter sermon. It was about the seven last words; he would take four of them, and I would alternate with three.

DMC—Dynamic Model of Consciousness

I was immensely flattered by the offer and I accepted immediately, although I didn't remember what the seven last words were.

Dave said he would come pick me up at 6am Easter morning. He lived near his church, about 30 miles away. Then, one week before Easter, he found me on campus and confirmed the arrangement. Yes, you'll pick me up at 6am.

How I suffered! I had two weeks to prepare, but I was haunted every day by the thought that Dave's four words would be brilliant and my three would suck. No matter what. How could I appear equal to a smart senior who had already been preaching for several years?

This panic left me helpless. Each day my fear increased. I didn't know what to do. I was too overwhelmed to even have it occur to me that I could go to the library and look something up.

Two weeks dragged by in the daytime and tormented me at night. And then Saturday night arrived. I hadn't been able to stop it. 6am was only 12 hours away.

I sank to my knees and did the only thing left. I prayed. Not that I felt my prayers had ever been answered before, but this moment was filled with desperation, so I prayed. Really hard.

God, get me out of this!! I don't care how you do it, just get me out of this!! I prayed in a continuous torrent.

DMC—Dynamic Model of Consciousness

I had never before prayed so pleadingly, so forcefully, so helplessly. I repeated my prayer again and again, twisting in agony, for thirty exhausting minutes, then set my alarm for 5:30 and collapsed in bed.

I got up, got cleaned and dressed, and went out front to wait for Dave. I did think he would show up and somehow save my ass, saying, Oh No, and grabbing a pen he would quickly write my part of the sermon.

Dave didn't show up. I was relieved, of course, to be off the hook for preaching, but I was also mystified. I just stayed inside the rest of the day blinking my eyes in wonderment.

It was Easter and the church was just down the street, but I had had enough Easter miracles for one day.

Then, Easter break was over which meant for one thing that I could eat again in the dining hall. My food was scarce during breaks.

It also meant that I could question Dave.

He was walking on the front campus and I went up to him. I said, You didn't pick me up Easter morning. He didn't seem to directly hear what I said, and responded, You know, the strangest thing happened the night before Easter. My car caught fire and burned up. So I've got a new car now, well, not new really but new to me!

I was knocked a little off balance because Dave didn't seem to recall our arrangement. I said, I was going to preach three of the seven last words.

Again, he heard only some of what I said. He chuckled and said, That's funny. Saturday night I realized that I hadn't finished my sermon. I still had three words to write about. So I stayed up pretty late and then my car caught fire.

Well. I was dumbfounded. I stood there stunned as Dave went on his way.

What had I triggered? My prayer had been answered all right, but I was staggered by the cost. What had I done? I destroyed a car and scrambled a man's brain just to get out of a speaking engagement.

I gave up praying after that, which for a student minister was unusual. I just didn't want the responsibility for the consequences.

I blamed the whole thing on God, of course. I didn't know then that it was I who was solely and entirely at fault, bearing full responsibility.

But I know that now, and so I am writing this book. I avoid religious terms like prayer. Prayer is only tenuously relevant to effective reality management techniques that are understood and available today.

I experienced a very significant demonstration of the creative power of consciousness with Dave. It was my intensely focused attention that enabled the answer to my prayer.

The DMC illustrates for you how this works.

The Non-Material Universe

Your understanding of the DMC relies on two agreements.

First, you agree that awareness exists as a real thing. Not believe, agree.

Belief in the existence of awareness is superfluous since awareness is your only genuinely first-hand reality and everything else is the stuff that you are aware of, the content passing through your awareness.

The second thing is, you agree to a single belief: the reality of frequency waves, that they exist, even though they are non-material, invisible, silent things.

This is not a difficult belief for you to accept in our era, with frequency waves evidencing themselves to you in a hundred ways every day, from your cell phone to your TV to your microwave.

But for eons, frequency waves were unsuspected. People believed that everything they saw was actually there.

The DMC illustrates how frequency waves are responsible for everything you experience. This phenomenon is one of the shocking recent discoveries that confront not only consciousness theorists but quantum physicists as well.

The DMC relies on the assumption that awareness exists as the primal thing. This is Awareness Theory.

From that assumption springs an algorithm that explains all of consciousness and all of reality, the DMC.

You can now view consciousness as a non-material thing, rather than as a feature of the physical brain.

Classical scientific method focuses on the study of the objective physical universe, which is why it investigates the physical brain in its search for consciousness.

Here's the voice of one prominent quantum physicist:

> But scientific method never ruled out the use of human consciousness as a variable. Mathematics and consciousness were both accepted as unquestioned fundamentals, but no thought seems to have been given to the acceptance of consciousness as a fundamental until the present century.
>
> Classical scientists still seem unaware that, in trying to apply scientific method to the discovery of consciousness in the brain, they have entered an area of investigation that is outside the scope of classical scientific method, because consciousness is a presumption of scientific method itself.

DMC—Dynamic Model of Consciousness

Consciousness cannot be studied objectively by classical scientific method because consciousness is itself being used in the attempt. Consciousness cannot be made a separate, objective thing to study; it cannot be studied without using the thing itself.

The universe is no longer seen as a machine, made up of a multitude of objects, but has to be pictured as one indivisible, dynamic whole whose parts are essentially interrelated and can be understood only as patterns of a cosmic process. [1]

Today's leading-edge physicists study a non-material universe. That includes our physical universe, now seen as non-material. This is quantum physics.

In modern physics, it has been discovered that what the scientist wishes to observe can determine what is observed, and so conscious awareness itself has become a part of the modern scientific process.

Modern physics no longer describes electrons as being material. Today's physicists tell us that particles and waves are two aspects of the same thing; particles are material and waves are non-material. Experiments show that what you look for, whether particles or waves, is what you see.

---

[1] Quoted from *The Tao of Physics* by Fritjof Capra.

DMC—Dynamic Model of Consciousness

Only waves exist until particles are detected by consciousness. Without contact with consciousness, it's all waves and no particles.[2]

Consciousness itself is a thing. According to quantum physics, the idea that material things exist in the universe is outdated. Every thing is fundamentally a non-material pattern.

Consciousness is a pattern, just like any and every other thing or reality.

The DMC stands as a validation of Awareness Theory.

---

[2] Quoted from Michael Talbot, *The Holographic Universe*

Dynamic Model of Consciousness

The DMC illustrates the core components of consciousness—awareness, intuition, attention, and [thought processing] mind; and the dynamic properties of each component.

These components work together to create our experience, whether sourced from outer or inner reality.

Understanding how our life experience is actually created allows us to actively manage the process, creating life experience of our choosing.

Ultimately, this can lead to the experience of enlightenment, although that is not the emphasis of this book.[3]

The DMC can be visualized in imagination and its dynamics mentally tracked.

That is, you can visualize frequency wave experience patterns being attracted to attention by resonance, being

---

[3] See my books *Mind Blow* and *Create Reality With Morphic Robots* for discussion of enlightenment.

interpreted by mind into experience, being intensified by attention and intuition, and delivered to awareness where the patterns are experienced as real.

This may all sound like nonsense at the moment, but there is a book ahead of you to explain it all.

Once you understand the DMC, it will change you. First, it more or less corners you with the concept that there is nothing material about material reality. That could be tough to accept, but it is quantum physics.

Understanding the DMC is greatly liberating, however, because your beliefs all become highly suspect, so much so that you will probably abandon them.

Suppose the universe really is made of nothing more substantial than numbers, as some scientists affirm.

Suppose the only way we can ever experience anything is to resonate with frequency waves.

Suppose the only time we can ever do something is in the ever-present now.

That is all good and correct supposing.

The DMC shows how this all works.

I will first describe each component of consciousness. Then I will assemble the DMC. Then I will describe its actions. Then, what it is good for, that is, how to make practical use of it to change what you want about your life.

Understanding Awareness

Awareness, as with each other core component, is considered in isolation. As we consider awareness, then, we must see it as empty, not aware of anything at all, just a power.

Physicists in many cases are acknowledging the necessity of including awareness in their interactions with particle realities.

That is, they say is there no reality out there until it resonates with some awareness somewhere, or in more immediate terms, until someone witnesses it (experiences it).

Without awareness, there is no reality, whether material or non-material, because according to quantum physics, nothing exists until it is experienced in awareness.

In fact, it is the very act of experiencing something that makes it real. Until it is experienced, it does not exist except as a maybe.

This positions awareness as the first principle of the universe. Awareness comes first. So before the Big Bang, there was awareness.

DMC—Dynamic Model of Consciousness

In the DMC, awareness is in the center. Experience patterns pass through your awareness.

Your personal universe consists of the frequency wave patterns that flow through your awareness.

That is, the entire universe that you experience exists, for you, only in your own awareness. It is like that for each of us; we each have our own personal version of the universe.

If you were to shut down your body senses, material reality, for you, would literally vanish because it is not resonating with your awareness. Gone in a blink.

Without your senses, you would still have experience patterns traveling to your awareness from both memories and other non-sensory sources.

The enlightenment experience is the experience of awareness only, isolated as a void without any experience content.

Thus, awareness can be experienced as a distinct thing in itself without any characteristics except its power of awareness. It is an independent freestanding entity.

Before science, people used their awareness to hunt for their souls, coming up empty-handed while their hands were full all along.

There is little more to say about awareness. We all have it and know exactly what it is. We know that awareness is real without any outside proof from science. Nor is awareness at all amenable to scientific scrutiny.

The important thing for present purposes is to visualize awareness as a single, freestanding component of consciousness, and not lump it into the general and undifferentiated concept we have been accustomed to: wrongly considering all of consciousness as one thing.

Figure 1 Awareness, shown existing alone without content.
Awareness is represented as a small dot at the center of the DMC.

DMC—Dynamic Model of Consciousness

Understanding Intuition

Figure 2 Intuition behaves like a crystal ball, and that is how it is represented in the DMC. It surrounds awareness.

Intuition is shown in the DMC as a clear crystal ball surrounding awareness at its center.

The intent here is to mimic the focusing effect that an actual crystal ball has on an image by condensing the image sharply at its center.

Intuition similarly focuses experience wave patterns down to sharp images in awareness.

This occurs after the patterns have already been partially focused by attention, which is what tailored them for entry to intuition in the first place; well, along with mind.

Patterns resonate with attention, get interpreted by mind, travel on through intuition, and explode into reality in awareness.

The function of intuition is simple. It further condenses frequency wave patterns down a sharp focus so you can experience them in awareness.

THE VOICE OF GOD

Some experience patterns come at you from angles other than the usual one that is in alignment with attention.

That is, there are occasional experience patterns that sidestep resonance with attention and mind, and hit intuition directly.

DMC—Dynamic Model of Consciousness

We call these sidesteppers intuitions, and you experience them without using your body's senses or your thought processes.

These unprocessed wave patterns simply pop into your awareness with a strange feeling, like this must certainly be the voice of God.

The strangeness is from experiencing a partially condensed pattern that bypassed your sensory input. It has not been partially condensed by attention, so it is not experienced with clarity.

DMC—Dynamic Model of Consciousness

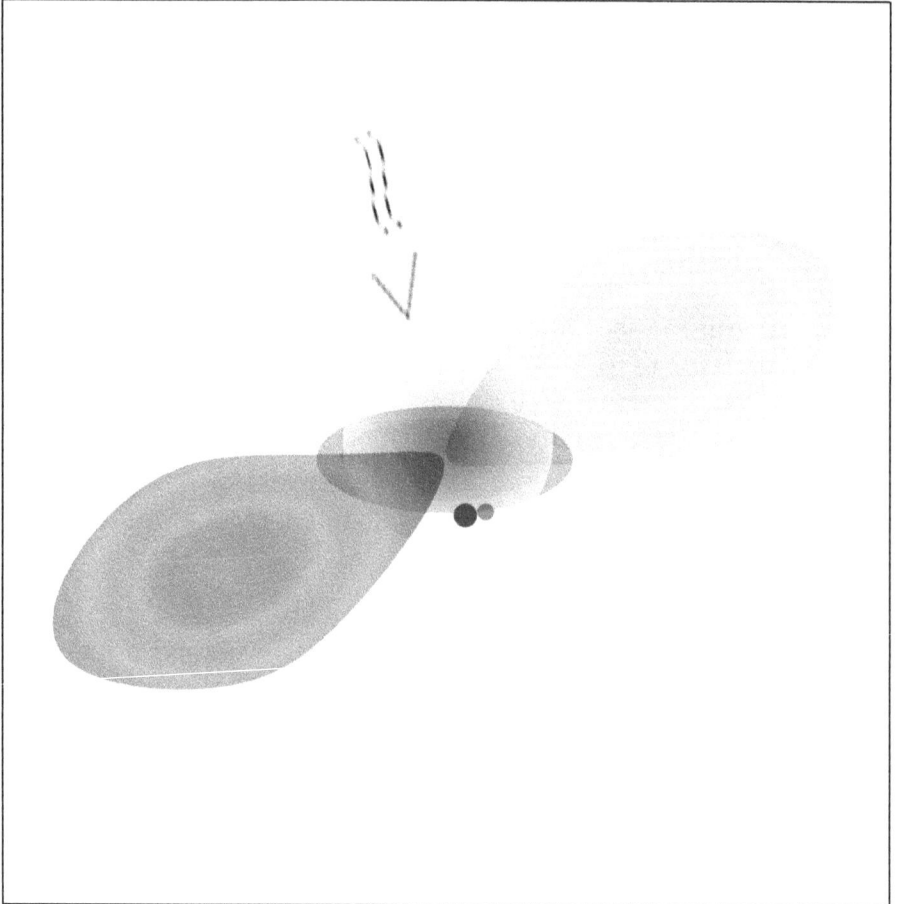

Figure 3 An experience pattern travels through intuition, bypassing attention and mind, creating a strange experience.

Understanding Attention

You know about attention. If you are awake, or even when you are dreaming, you are paying attention.

In the DMC, attention is represented as a sphere that orbits around intuition.

Its rapid orbit forms a disc-shaped field. This field behaves like an antenna for patterns.

It is your attention that delimits awareness of infinite possibilities down to a manageable individual slice: the patterns aligned with the disc-shaped field.

Resonance becomes possible with patterns that reach you by entering the disc field from its outer edge so that they travel through the wedge of the disc's shrinking radius.

This disc shape assures that the shrinking radius of the circular field condenses the experience pattern as it approaches intuition.

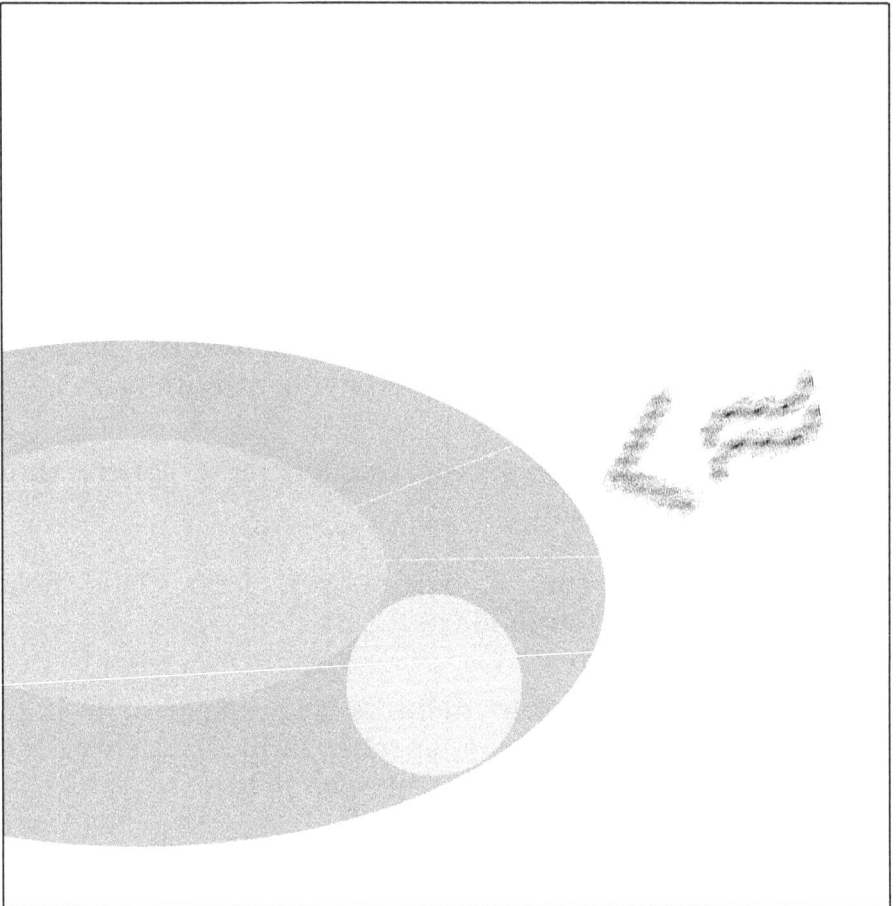

Figure 4 An experience pattern in its normal expanded state approaches a wedge-shaped area of attention's field where it is condensed.

It is your attention that looks for and pays attention to things, and this activity generates brain waves that seek resonance with harmonious counterparts, namely, patterns that produce the experience sought.

Mostly, your attention finds these patterns in memory. For anything that you want to continue to exist, perhaps the chair you are sitting in, the memory, a frequency wave pattern that produces your chair, repeatedly passes through your attention at a speed so fast that you don't notice the interstitial instances when the chair stops existing.

It is your attention that is resonating with the chair memory so that it will be recalled to your now, the present moment. On every orbit, attention repeats the resonant contact.

In some instances, new experience patterns are attracted to and by attention; that is, they resonate. This most often occurs when you seek something.

These outside patterns become additions to your memory storehouse by traveling through your attention, mind, intuition, awareness, and then becoming memory.

DMC—Dynamic Model of Consciousness

Understanding Mind, the Thought Processor

In the DMC, mind means pattern processor, or what we call thinker. The word mind is often used to refer to consciousness in general. But not here.

Mind is represented as a sphere in orbit around attention. On every orbit it passes through attention's disc-shaped field, where it interprets the patterns that are in resonance with attention.

The DMC describes mind as a means of interpreting patterns, only. Mind compares the patterns entering attention with the contents of the Alpha cloud of previous experiences, and when it finds matches or similarities, it shares them with attention.

Attention condenses and passes them along to intuition for further condensation and then to awareness for the experience.

The activity of mind is not inherent but is regulated by attention. Attention is the only part of your consciousness that you can actively manage, and you use it to direct your mind.

DMC—Dynamic Model of Consciousness

For purposes of changing your experience of reality, you would deliberately fabricate thoughts for your mind to think.

Your mind will think what you tell it to think because the frequency waves you emit for a particular experience are the same, whether the experience is previously real or is newly made up.

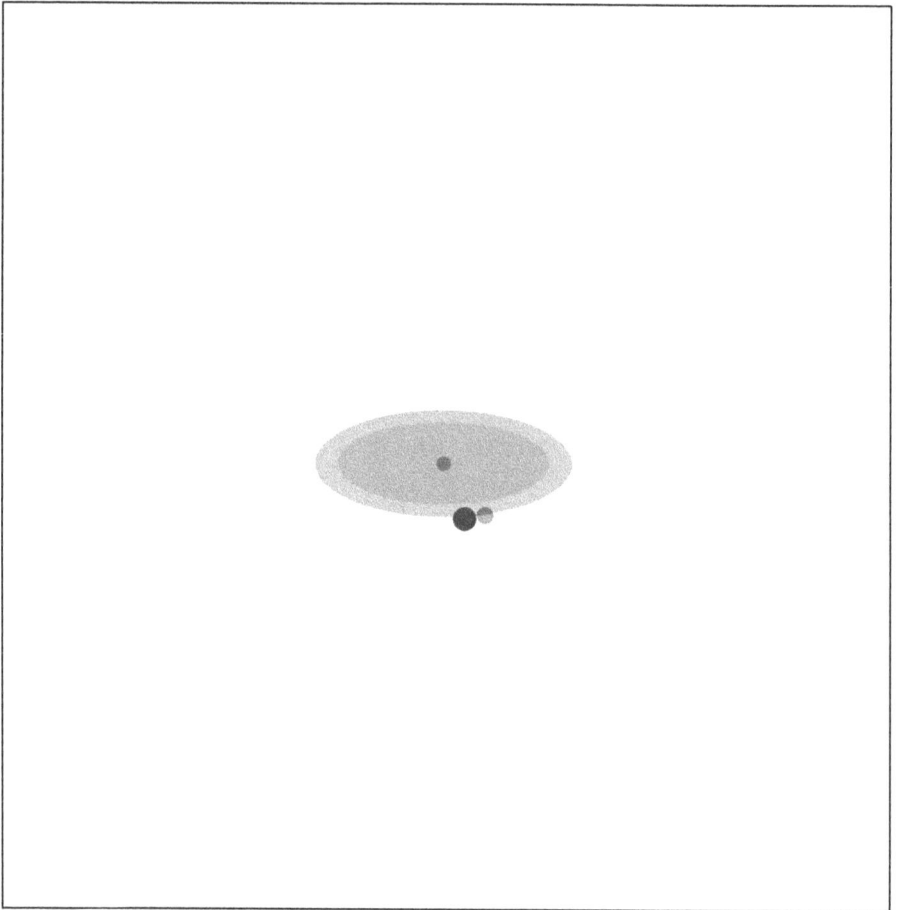

Figure 5 Mind orbits attention.

Your Past and Future

The only time you have that is real is now, this instant. You can recall past memories but you do the recalling now.

In the DMC, memories (your past) are shown in a cloud of traveling patterns. This part of your consciousness system is not conscious until you pull some of it into now.

This cloud is termed Alpha, after its dominant brainwave patterns that generate experience patterns such as memories, imagination, daydreaming, etc.

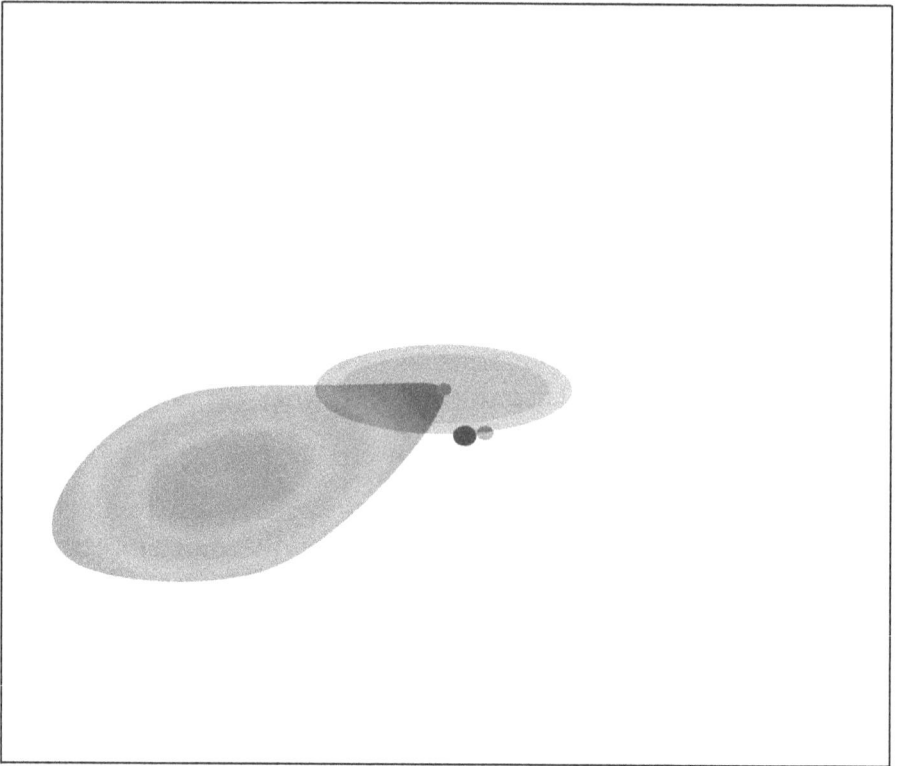

Figure 6 The Alpha cloud of past experience patterns.

In the DMC, the future is shown in a similar cloud of patterns, all potential realities. Most of these future patterns have gotten there by traveling from your past.

The future cloud is termed Beta, representing the brainwave patterns that generate experience of material reality.

Again, the clouds are made of uncountable frequency wave patterns that fly around the infinity loop, bypassing awareness on their entry to Beta because of low resonance, and triggering experiences in awareness as they return to Alpha.

30

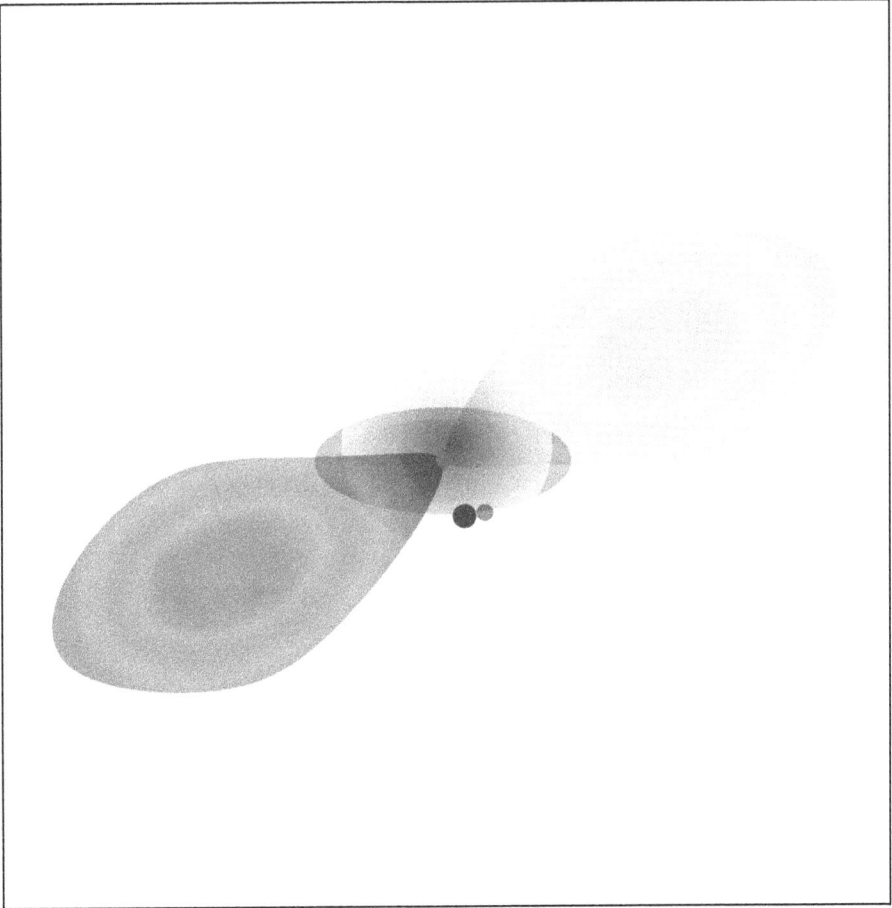

Figure 7 Adding the Beta cloud of future experience patterns completes the DMC.

With the future cloud in place, we can see an infinity loop/figure-eight travel pattern.

DMC—Dynamic Model of Consciousness

A memory pattern travels in the Alpha cloud until it reaches the center point of awareness, then enters the future cloud and travels through to awareness again.

The Flow of Experience Patterns

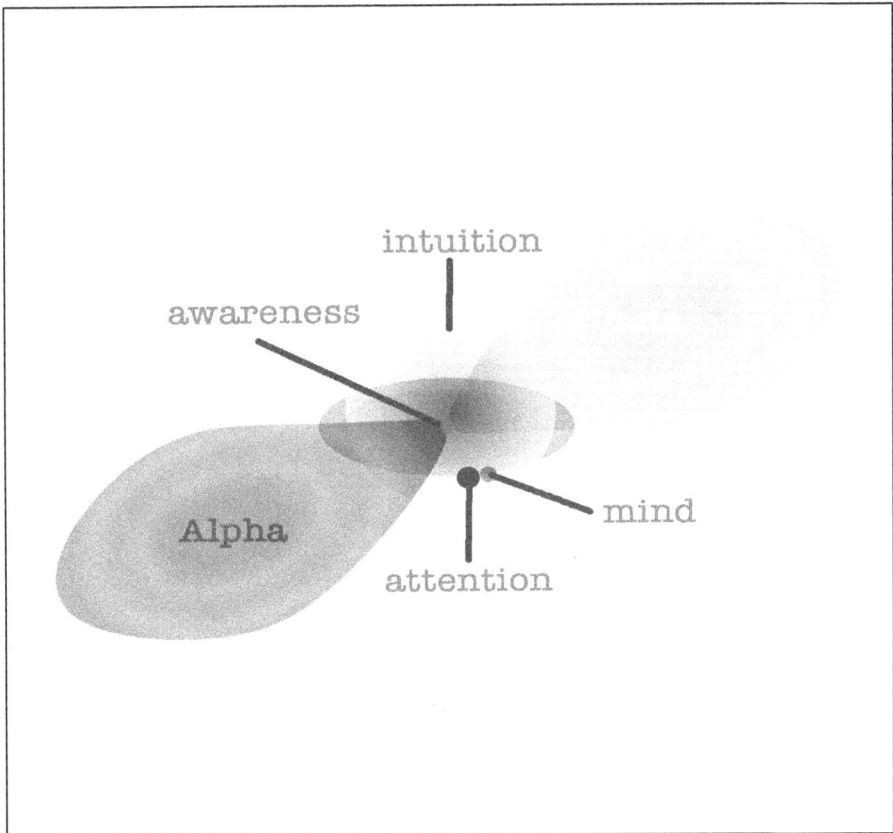

Figure 8 The assembled DMC.

DMC—Dynamic Model of Consciousness

An experience pattern generates your experience of something as a reality. It derives from your Alpha cloud of remembered patterns; and/or, it derives from some of the infinite chaos outside of your memory store.

A pattern typically enters awareness from Beta, the store of patterns we call the future. It resonates with attention,

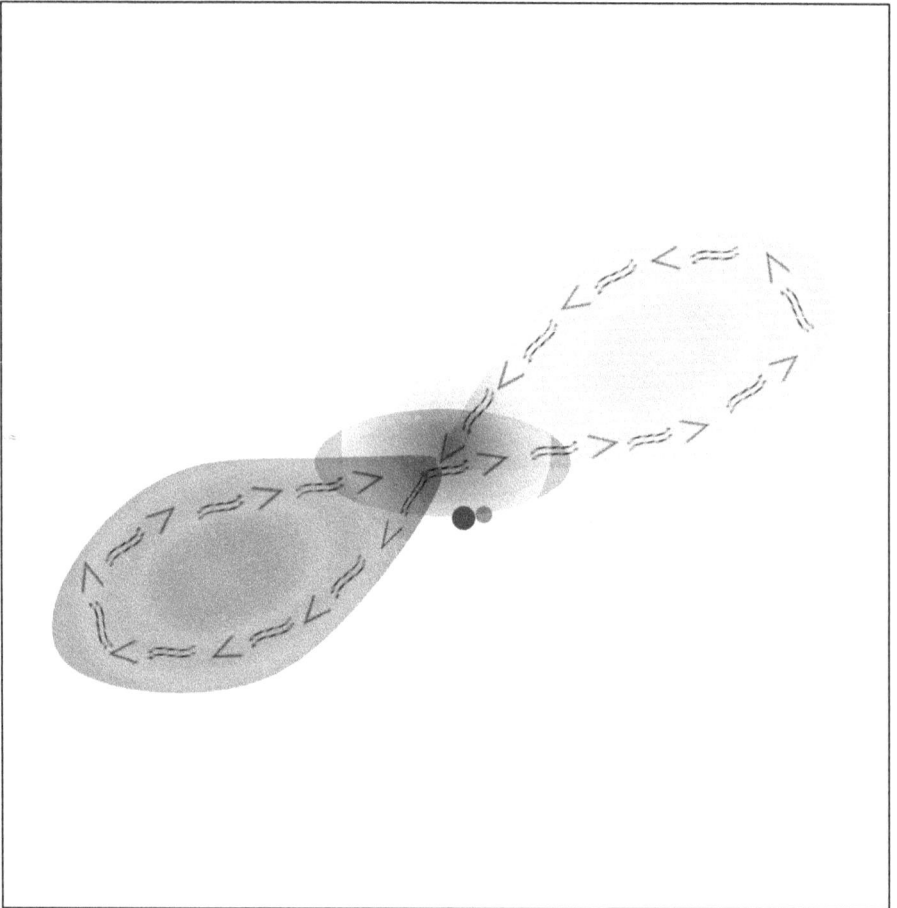

Figure 9 Visualize an experience wave pattern traveling through your consciousness system.

DMC—Dynamic Model of Consciousness

is interpreted by mind, is condensed by intuition, and bursts into reality as it travels through awareness.

In the DMC, a pattern approaches awareness from the Beta cloud, and after passing through attention and mind and intuition and awareness, it emerges from awareness into the Alpha cloud and is stored as a memory.

The pattern then returns to the Beta cloud (when summoned by resonance) by following the infinity loop.

When attention seeks to resonate with something not found in the Alpha store, it reaches beyond and, upon fulfilling the rules of resonance, resonates with something new.

DMC—Dynamic Model of Consciousness

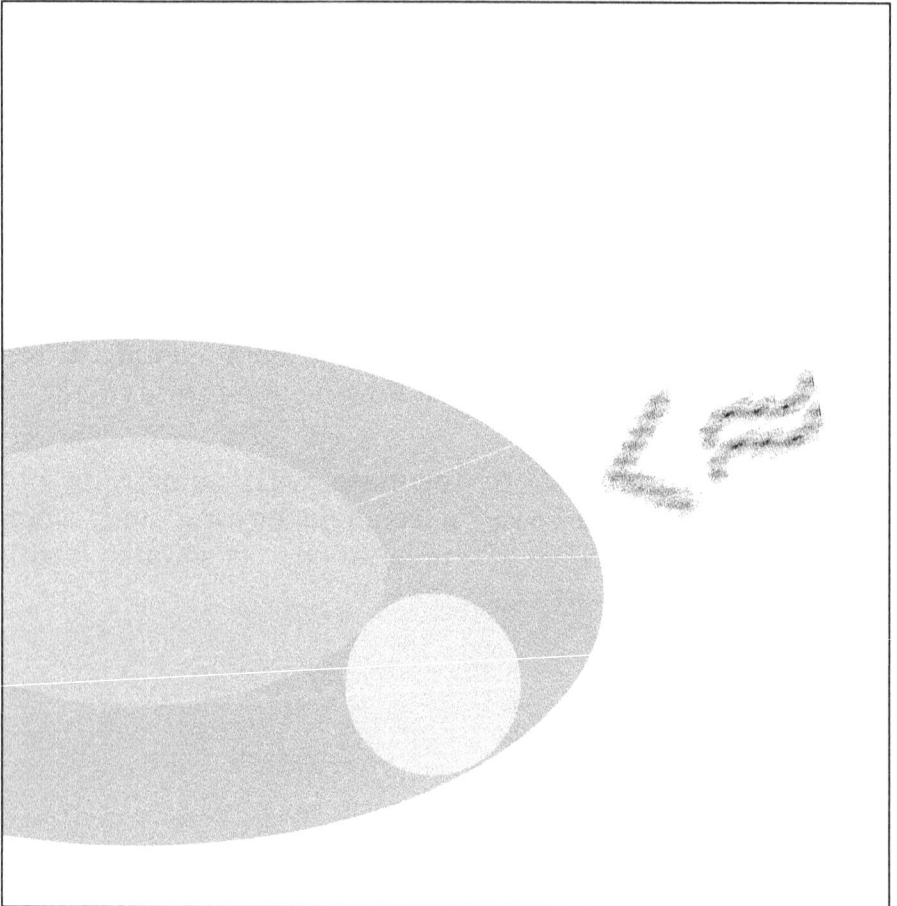

Figure 10 An experience pattern in its normal expanded state approaches a wedge-shaped area of attention's field.

DMC—Dynamic Model of Consciousness

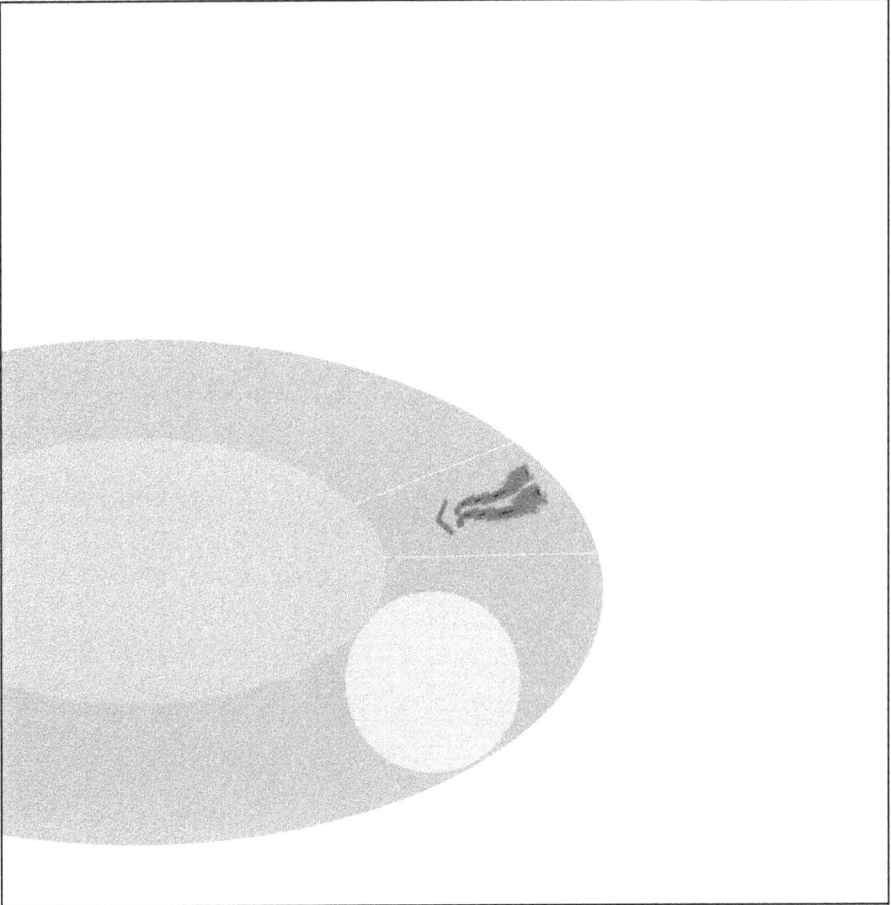

Figure 11 The experience pattern is condensed as it passes through the wedge-shaped section of the disc field.

DMC—Dynamic Model of Consciousness

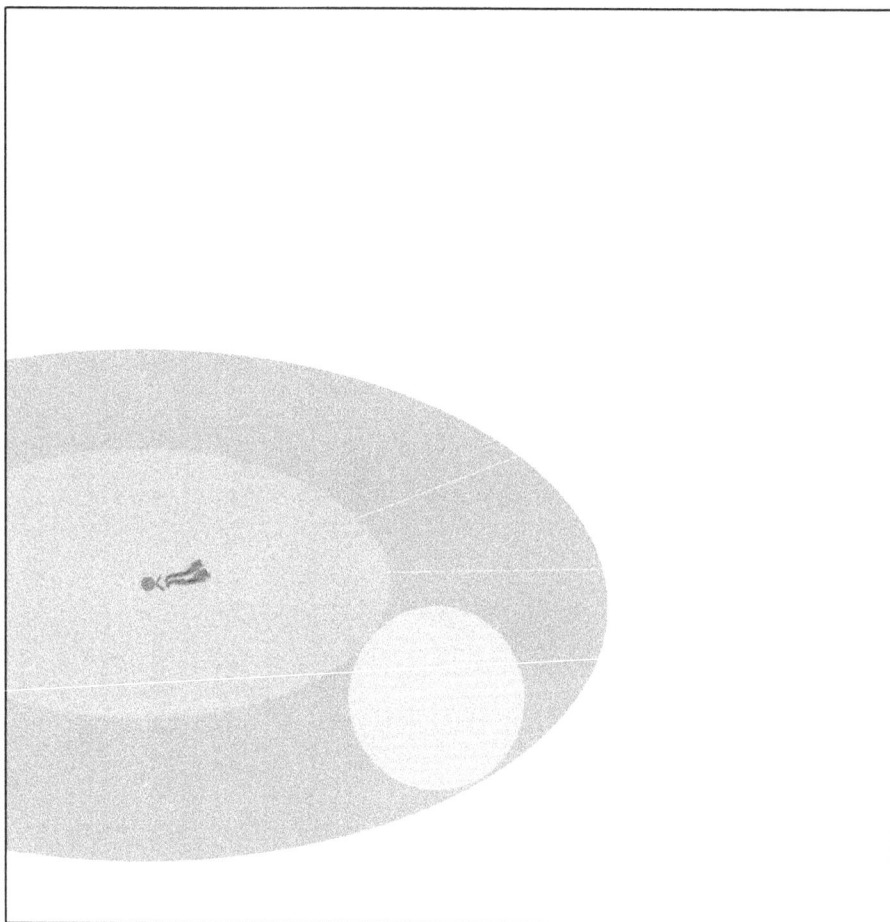

Figure 12 Intuition further condenses the pattern down to awareness, where it is experienced.

DMC—Dynamic Model of Consciousness

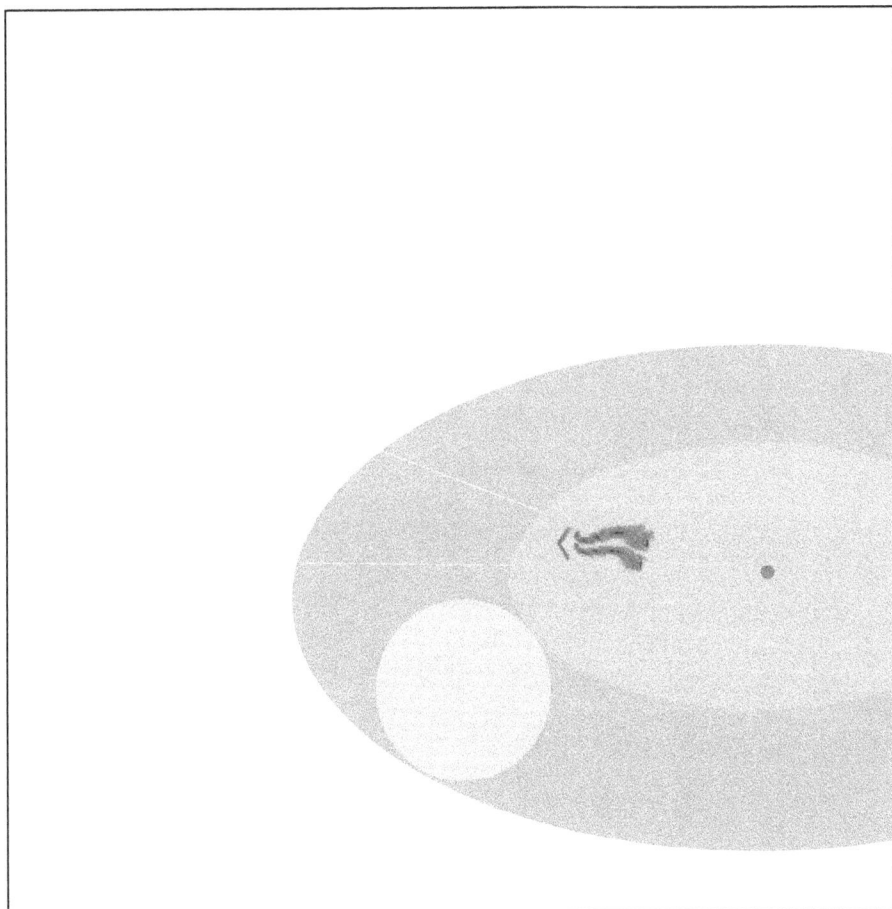

Figure 13 The experience pattern exits awareness, and intuition expands it.

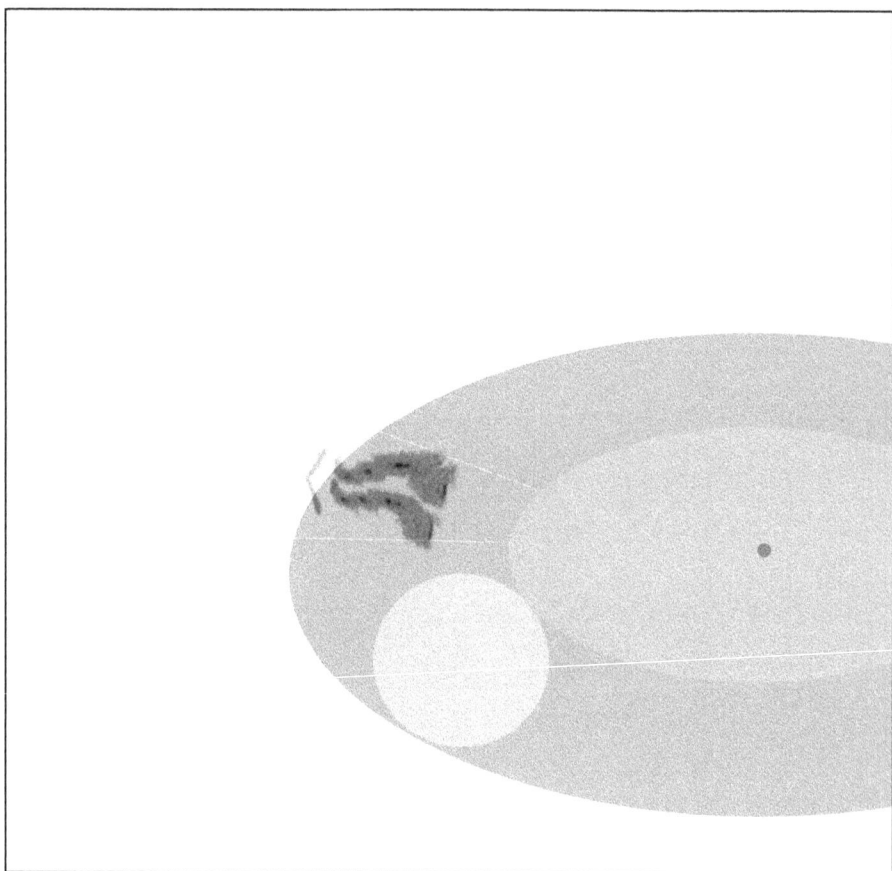

Figure 14 The experience pattern exits intuition and the attention field expands it to its normal state.

Understanding Frequency Wave Behaviors

Dan Russell at Penn State has created an excellent series of animations demonstrating frequency wave behaviors. I have drawn the following details from his valuable work, which is at:

http://www.acs.psu.edu/drussell/demos.html

When it sinks in that your experience is generated by frequency waves, you can understand the possibilities that you are dealing with by working with frequency waves on their level.

Suppose something is constantly bothering you. You can understand that this is resonance between your own consciousness system and the incoming frequency wave pattern.

So stop the resonance and you will stop the bothering thing. Resonance can be stopped because traveling frequency waves can be changed into standing frequency waves that aren't resonating with anything.

DMC—Dynamic Model of Consciousness

The polarity of a traveling wave can be changed between positive and negative. That is another clue that negative or positive experience patterns can be changed.

A barrier can bounce back or redirect a frequency wave and change its amplitude or its polarity or its frequency in the process.

Simply knowing that frequency waves are changeable in several ways builds confidence that the frequency wave patterns creating your experience can be changed.

I believe that even a little understanding of these behaviors will be directly applicable to your change projects. Dr. Russell's animations are a treasure for anyone wanting an understanding of frequency wave behaviors.

Deja-vu

THE ATHOL LIBRARY SHIMMERS

I came home from school, checked in, and headed right back out. I was walking to the library to do my homework.

I started to cross the broad intersection in front of the library. I looked at the library and it suddenly trembled and shimmered and I knew that I had seen this exact view before. I remembered it clearly.

This experience was a great puzzle to me. I wanted to look it up in the library, but I didn't know what to look up.

> **déjà vu** *noun* /deɪ ʒɑˈvu/ the strange feeling that in some way you have already experienced what is happening now[4]

The DMC can make sense of déjà vu.

Suppose some force nudges an incoming experience pattern as it enters the attention disc, and the nudge pushes the pattern aside a little so that, instead of

---

[4] Definition of "déjà vu" from the Cambridge Academic Content Dictionary © Cambridge University Press

entering the attention disc squarely aligned, it is misaligned. The part that is not aligned bypasses attention and mind. It continues on directly to intuition.

Meanwhile, the other part of the pattern is being processed normally and that causes it to arrive a bit later. The total pattern passes through awareness twice, in two parts, and that creates the deja-vu effect.

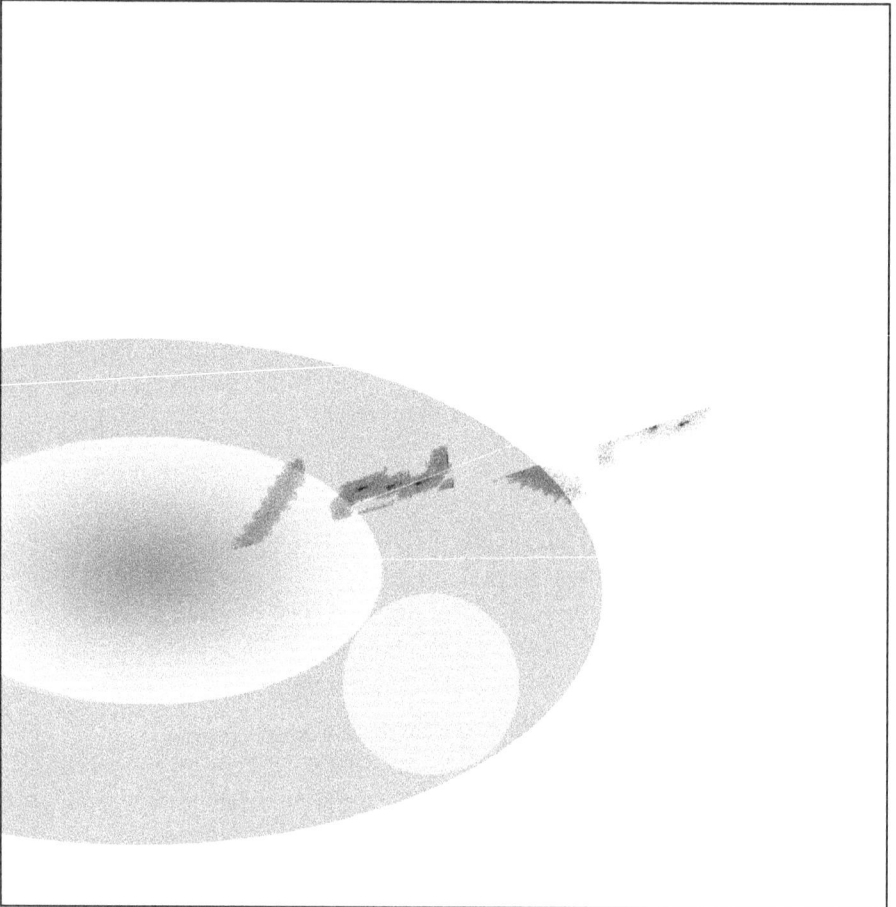

Figure 15 Deja-vu. An experience pattern splits and one part bypasses attention, arriving at awareness sooner than the other part that is delayed by attention and mind processing.

Understanding Synchronicity

The impressive manner by which waves seek and find resonance with other waves and create new realities is called synchronicity or surprising coincidence.

Synchronicity, in philosophy, is the experience of two or more events that are causally unrelated, yet are experienced as occurring together in a meaningful manner. Carl Jung first described it in the 1920s.[5]

Here are a few examples. Remember that synchronicity occurs when the rules of resonance have been fulfilled.

THE ICE CREAM CONE

I was teaching a small group in my studio apartment. I hadn't yet suffered through the four years I later devoted to developing the algorithm for the DMC, but I knew the components and could talk about them.

---

[5]https://en.wikipedia.org/wiki/Synchronicity_(disambiguation)

DMC—Dynamic Model of Consciousness

I was explaining how we create our reality by sending out brainwaves.

As a demonstration, I suggested that we each create something simple. I thought about ice cream, thus generating brain waves about ice cream. I told them my creation was ice cream and that I had felt the word move across the front of my head.

The group continued for perhaps another hour, and we had all forgotten about the demonstration. When we broke up for the evening, we lingered on the sidewalk, talking some more.

Just then, my landlady walked up and was holding two ice cream cones. George, she said, do you want an ice cream? I bought one for my husband but he doesn't want it.

The group was stunned and looking at each other, except me because I wanted the ice cream.

Did this demonstration meet the rules of resonance?

It was a simple experience to create. Ice cream was available in the convenience store next door. It was not far-fetched to imagine that by some means ice cream could appear. Resonance was entirely possible.

I gave little power to this creation. I did give it my intense focus for the moment, and it seems that was enough.

We were all focusing on our own thing, sitting quietly together for perhaps 30 seconds. That seems a short time to qualify as consistency, but for a little creation like ice cream, it was enough. My Dave prayer may have been way too long at 30 minutes.

One woman in the group later told me that she had created for her experiment, success for her real estate business, which had been in the doldrums for some time. After our meeting, she said she began closing sales one after another.

This phenomenon of creating reality is produced by attention concentrating on the desired result. Attention broadcasts waves that find harmonious waves to resonate with.

Attention broadcasts waves without necessarily using the senses. Attention receives waves through the senses, however.

A recent study shows that people born blind can learn to see through their other senses. Their quality of vision is comparable to a sighted person's peripheral vision.

REBECCA AND THE SPARK

I was once again starting my life over. I was in El Paso and decided to return to Boston and write. I had less than a hundred dollars and my belongings had been reduced to a suitcase. I got a drive away car, which cost me only gasoline to make the trip.

I rented the cheapest room I could find, signed up with a temp agency, and started earning some money. The fourth floor of the building I was in had a studio apartment. I fixed it up and moved in.

On Christmas Eve, I threw a party for the residents of the building who were mostly alcoholic, addicted, and mentally ill people. Then on Christmas day, another party started and I was invited.

Rebecca sat across the room. We hadn't spoken. When our eyes met, a spark flew between our eyes, visible to both of us, and it was one of the first things we talked about. We both saw it. It was bright. It was mind rattling.

This was dramatic resonance, two fields immediately resonating on contact. We needed no conversation, no dating, nothing more. The resonance had been established.

You can call that love at first sight if you wish. Love is actually strong resonance, so that is what I call it.

MOMMY LEARNS ENGLISH

My mother's family moved from Quebec to Vermont when she was in fourth grade. She didn't know a word of English.

She found herself in an English-speaking school where she felt lost. But she was determined to learn English.

She told me that she paid close attention to the speech of the other students for two weeks, and then she could suddenly speak English. It happened in an instant.

At the time, I was really amazed by her story. However, it is another example of creating reality by fulfilling the rules of resonance.

The possibility of learning English, of establishing resonance with English, was readily at hand, meeting the first rule.

Mommy had to learn English. She really had no choice about it, and she needed to do it fast so she wouldn't fall behind in school, a serious embarrassment for a good student.

The matter was urgent, stimulating a pressured outpouring of power sufficient to establish the resonance, meeting the second rule.

She persisted for two weeks, every moment every day, and then the resonance was suddenly established, meeting the third rule.

From that moment, she spoke English as well as her classmates.

THE HOUSE OF HELL'S ANGELS

The rental office refused my rent because I was a day late. They didn't mention the two dogs I cared for that upset the apartment complex with their constant barking, but I suppose that was the real reason.

So I had to move. At this stage of my life, I simply expected solutions to my problems to magically appear, and they did. It was my creative power to survive, on autopilot.

Now I needed a place to live. I didn't know what to do about it, having no resources at the time.

On the night before my move-out date, a friend stopped by and said she was staying with a friend in a house owned by the Hell's Angels motorcycle club, and I could move in because they were seldom around.

So I moved during the night and lived there for a while.

They did stop by one night and I got to meet several of the Hell's Angels.

The Rules of Resonance

Resonance comes from radiation between two frequency wave fields.

Simply put, radiation is frequency waves stimulating resonance in another field that then radiates waves.

The usual demonstration of resonance is done with two identical tuning forks. One is struck and sings. It is brought close to the other, and that starts the other tuning fork singing, or resonating.

For resonance to occur between two wave fields, three rules apply.

RESONANT RULE

Both fields must be capable of resonating on the same frequencies.

The potential for harmony is required. Without it, fields cannot connect; they remain in the pool of chaos. Only those will be available to you that find harmony or resonance with patterns in your Alpha and Beta stores.

POWER RULE

The power or amplitude of your resonance must be strong enough to stimulate resonance in the other field.

Power here refers to the amplitude of a field of frequency waves. Amplitude can be increased by concentrating attention, and by painting with emotion.

CONSISTENCY RULE

You must persist until resonance is established.

Your strong resonance must be directed continuously until resonance in the other field has been stimulated (homeostasis overcome).

When these three rules are satisfied, resonance occurs, whether you like it or not.

Consider now my earlier story about Dave. Did my hyper-prayer meet the rules of resonance? It is only by meeting the three rules of resonance that the prayer would be answered.

My prayer met the resonant rule. It was pointed to a possibility that already existed in my reality: cancelling my appearance.

My prayer very definitely met the power rule. The focus and emotion I poured into that prayer was huge.

And, in hindsight, the prayer met the consistency rule, meaning that my half hour of such intense prayer was enough to trigger appropriate wave fields into resonance.

I had prayed: I don't care how you do it, just get me out of this. That left a lot of possibilities open. Wave fields went to work, coordinating possibilities into synchronicities and generating results.

You can deal with anything at all when you work at the level of waves. And that is the new paradigm view of reality.

EMOTION IS AMPLITUDE

Emotion does not appear in the DMC except as an add-in because emotion is not a component of consciousness.

Emotion is a wave's amplitude, how high and low the waves are. The higher the wave's amplitude is, the more powerfully you experience the pattern, whether that is positive or negative.

Amplitude can be modified as suggested in the chapter Frequency Wave Behaviors, possibly addressing many problem emotions.

Other writers will no doubt contribute further on this topic; it is not for me.

Your Brain Wavebands

Since I first began writing about brain wavebands, the definitions and number of bands have changed at least three times.

First, there were four wavebands and common dreaming occurred in Theta and lucid dreaming occurred in Delta.

Then, lucid dreaming was moved to Theta.

Then, a fifth waveband was added, Mu, where nothing much happens, with frequencies of 8-12 Hz.

Then came Gamma waves (38 TO 42 Hz).

Gamma brainwaves are the fastest brain waves (high frequency, like a flute), and relate to simultaneous processing of information from different brain areas.

Gamma brainwaves pass information rapidly, and as the subtlest of the brainwave frequencies, the mind has to be quiet to access it.

Gamma is also above the frequency of neuronal firing, so how it is generated remains a mystery.

DMC—Dynamic Model of Consciousness

It is speculated that Gamma rhythms modulate perception and consciousness, and that a greater presence of Gamma relates to expanded consciousness and spiritual emergence.

In their EEG tests, researchers have confirmed that you can have all or a combination of your brainwaves active at the same time, although with one band dominating.

Table 1 lists the various brainwaves and their frequency wave ranges, according to recent research. I recently observed that this growing list has spawned two sub-ranges, so it seems not to be a settled matter yet.

TABLE COMPARISON OF EEG BANDS[6]

Band	Frequency (Hz)	Location	Normally
Delta	< 4	frontally in adults, posteriorly in children; high-amplitude waves	• adult slow-wave sleep • in babies • Has been found during some continuous-attention tasks[46]
Theta	4 – 7	Found in locations not related to task at hand	• higher in young children • drowsiness in adults and teens • idling • Associated with inhibition of

---

[6] https://en.wikipedia.org/wiki/Electroencephalography#Wave_patterns

			elicited responses (has been found to spike in situations where a person is actively trying to repress a response or action).[46]
Alpha	8 – 15	posterior regions of head, both sides, higher in amplitude on dominant side. Central sites (c3-c4) at rest	• relaxed/reflecting • closing the eyes • Also associated with inhibition control, seemingly with the purpose of timing inhibitory activity in different locations across the brain.
Beta	16 – 31	both sides, symmetrical distribution, most evident frontally; low-amplitude waves	• range span: active calm -> intense -> stressed -> mild obsessive • active thinking, focus, hi alert, anxious
Gamma	32 +	Somatosensory cortex	• Displays during cross-modal sensory processing (perception that combines two different senses, such as sound and sight)[47][48] • Also is shown during short-term memory matching of recognized objects, sounds, or tactile sensations

Mu	8 – 12	Sensorimotor cortex	• Shows rest-state motor neurons.[7][49]

These data form a scale from <4Hz to 32+Hz. Delta is the slowest and Gamma is the fastest.

Another way to look at this scale is as a density scale, with Gamma being the least dense and Delta the most dense.

Gamma is the fastest and the least dense, having little or no resonance with materiality patterns.

Delta is the slowest and densest, having very high resonance with materiality patterns.

The slower the brainwave, the greater the density of the experience pattern.

LaBerge's research into lucid dreaming[8] proved that lucid dreams occur in the Delta waveband. Recalling that some people describe lucid dreams as more real than real, this would be the high-density experience expected from the above.

We are interested here in the several alternate worlds that we can experience. Based on experience, you can assign a relative degree of density to the various wavebands.

---

[8] LaBerge is mentioned further in the next chapter.

DMC—Dynamic Model of Consciousness

For example, you already know that Alpha's reality of imagination and daydreaming is not as dense or real as things are in Beta.

You know that your experience of the everyday material world comes from Beta waves.

Counterintuitive as it may appear, your usual real world, Beta, is not your most real reality. Daydreams, followed by common dreams, are both more real when measured by density.

This may be fascinating, but I am more intent on its implications for exploring alternate worlds.

I will speak of four worlds that you can experience: Material World, Dream World, Lucid Dream World, and Awareness World.

DMC—Dynamic Model of Consciousness

Understanding the Alternate Reality Wavebands

MATERIAL WORLD

I have called your experience of material reality Beta. This term, along with Alpha, does seem to be established. Beta waveband is the one you use the most, assuming you are mostly awake.

Also recognize that your Alpha experiences partner with Beta, giving you imaginative input, and that you balance these two every day, letting one dominate, then the other.

You can recognize now that Beta is also an alternate reality since it occurs in the same consciousness system and in the same way as the other wavebands.

DREAM WORLD

The laws of physics are quite different in the Dream World.

There is gravity holding things down, but gravity is optional for the dreamer. The dreamer can fly.

Time exists in scenario packets and things vanish instead of continuing to exist as they do in Beta. Things don't last long.

Mind functions at a greatly reduced level, providing very little critical analysis of anything, making even the most absurd dreams believable.

Most common dreams occur in the Theta waveband.

LUCID DREAM WORLD

In the lucid dream state, the Beta mind awakens during the common dream and renders the dream scene in scintillating vividness, creating some of life's most exciting experiences. Some describe it as more real than real.

Skilled lucid dreamers learn to create custom dream adventures. Anything that you can imagine, you can create in a lucid dream.

I recommend the lucid dreaming books by Stephen LaBerge, a pioneer at Stanford University's Lucidity Institute.

AWARENESS WORLD

Awareness itself exists alone as an empty void. When your attention escapes from resonance with all wavebands of experience patterns, leaving only your empty awareness, you find yourself in the void of the universe, pure awareness.

This is the enlightenment or self-realization experience alluded to in the remarks on Gamma waves. Just imagine—you now know the frequency range for enlightenment.

The enlightenment experience is significant because it shows you that your awareness, your real self, doesn't die, even if you leave absolutely everything behind. You cannot possibly leave yourself behind. No more fear.

Enlightenment is an experience, not a belief or a state of mind.

After you have the experience, your state of mind will be different, and that is an effect of enlightenment. Fear will be gone, along with most stress, most anxiety, etc.

DMC—Dynamic Model of Consciousness

How the Universe Began

Everything experienced reduces to frequency waves, and frequency waves are really numbers.

Numbers come from, it appears to me, the Fibonacci Sequence, which means there have to be two number ones to get the sequence started.

One one sprang from awareness, that, from awareness by itself and without content, existing as the one and only thing, a clear case of a one.

Awareness became aware of an object that was not itself: its ability or power to be aware.

That makes two ones. The first is awareness, aware only of its own existence. The second is the power or ability to host content (experience something).

The two number ones resonate with awareness, since they are timelessly suspended in awareness. Aware of each other, then, the two ones did something numbers can do; they added themselves together, producing a new number, two.

Let the Sequence begin.

DMC—Dynamic Model of Consciousness

The Big Bang was this division of awareness into two things, triggering the Fibonacci Sequence and the resulting instant creation of a mathematical model of our universe.

Numbers have no motion, but since they are pure abstractions that exist everywhere at once, they don't need motion to interact. That is why the Bang was Big. It happened everywhere at once.

When numbers began describing waves, that created a mode of travel, and equations traveled in waves, seeking resonance.

Dealing with reality as waves is one level removed from the level of pure numbers, but that is not bad. It puts you where the action is.

As opposed to numbers that do not change, with waves all you get is change, a constant flow of changing waves.

Using the DMC

All of the experience patterns you can imagine are out there in the universe of waves, waiting for your call.

Your call, of course, is the brainwave patterns that you generate by concentration.

You have an endless supply of brainwaves. Go fishing for experiences.

To generate the brainwaves for your pattern, think your pattern, imagine your pattern.

You want to generate brainwaves for a cup of coffee? Concentrate on coffee and that creates the brainwaves for you.

If you can't formulate a clear pattern, but you do have a clear intention, try just concentrating on the words.

Recall my story about the ice cream cone. I imagined the words, ice cream, not a picture of ice cream itself. I saw the words, made of letters, cross above my forehead.

The DMC has no moral hindrances. Awareness is simply there. Numbers and waves are simply there. You don't need any beliefs and you don't need to accept any limitations.

Anything you can imagine can be created. However, if you want to create a unicorn, that may take you a while.

Realize that what you want to create will be assembled using patterns that, working together, result in your creation. If those patterns are readily available in your slice of the universe, your results can be swift.

Fulfill the rules of resonance and your patterns will manifest in your experience.

About the Author

Occupations, relationships, persona, locales, all flash by in the merry, complicated life of George Arthur Lareau.

Lareau's workdays began at age eight as a shoeshine boy, on the sidewalks and in the bars of Athol, MA. His business was successful enough to provide the groceries for his family for several years.

As a high school senior in Athol, he was president of seven organizations. He was a licensed Methodist minister at age 16, the youngest in New England, and served as assistant minister of St. Matthew's Methodist Church in Belleville, Illinois, while in college.

He was a Boston beatnik poet at age 19 and sold his first book, *The Hunting Poise*, on the sidewalks of Boston. He had several short-lived jobs during his beatnik years:

He sold a lot of encyclopedias door-to-door and bought his first new car.

DMC—Dynamic Model of Consciousness

He was director of advertising for United Trading Stamp Company in Boston at age 20, having started at the lowest clerical level six months earlier.

He was a dispatcher for Gaghan & Shaw appliance repair company in Washington, D.C. while living with a family from India. He then rode a bicycle back to Boston, which took him eleven days.

After this busy two-year hiatus, he finished studies for his Bachelor's degree in English and philosophy at McKendree University and married at age 23 in Amboy, IL.

In Amboy, he operated a small printing shop, and then was a child welfare social worker in Rockford, Illinois.

He studied acting in college and starred in two plays. He acted in and directed plays and theatres in Lebanon, Amboy and Freeport, IL.

He edited the company magazine for Burgess Battery Company in Freeport, IL, and then moved to Champaign, IL.

In Champaign-Urbana he built an ad agency that served an impressive list of clients in downstate Illinois.

He produced and directed films and TV commercials, produced and hosted a radio show, produced an audio-visual in Delhi, India, published a poetry anthology, free-lanced as a writer-photographer, was a city beat news reporter for the *Champaign-Urbana News Gazette*, edited two trade magazines owned a print and silkscreen shop, published a photography trade magazine, and was president of the Chicago chapter of ASMP (American Society of Media Photographers). He was also an Urbana city department commissioner.

He was next an estate and financial planner with American Express and authored financial planning software.

He established a major group for an Indian guru in Urbana, IL (Ruhani Satsang).

He founded a new religion chartered in Arizona (CNASRA, Church of the New Age Spiritual Revolution of America).

In other moves around the country, he sang classical music professionally in St. Petersburg, FL, El Paso, TX, and Boston, MA.

He was a systems analyst for the Mass. Dept. of Public Health in Boston, also for McDonnell-Douglas Helicopter Co. in Mesa, AZ, and worked nine telemarketing jobs in between writing books.

For two years he taught English and managed a foreigners guesthouse in Tokyo. Later, he taught English for six years in Beijing and managed the largest English school in China.

DMC—Dynamic Model of Consciousness

In his search for truth about the nature of reality and consciousness, he read over 5000 books, experimented with dozens of paths, and made many personal discoveries.

He analyzed the ways that truth is created and wrote *Three Peaks, a Model for Understanding Truth.*

He pursued mystical enlightenment and while in Boston achieved an enlightenment experience compatible with both the new physics and historical metaphysics.

Returning to Arizona, he worked once again as a child protective services worker, and built a substantial eBay camera business.

He created Sufi George, authored several books and built a popular web site, taught classes, made radio and television appearances and gave speeches.

He created over 60 cartoons that are on youtube.com.

He is now the Head Teacher of SGM's American Zen Monastery, a center for activities that promote freedom from belief and religion in favor of a science-based approach to reality and the achievement of enlightenment--American Zen.

Other Books by the Author

Search amazon.com for: George Arthur Lareau *for a complete listing.*

The Truth At Last! A Discourse on Generated Reality

Mind Blow: Understanding Consciousness

Create Reality with Morphic Robots

Three Peaks: A Model for Understanding Truth

A Chat with the Devil: Short Fiction

The Game Is Played on a Delicate Foundation, and even better poems

Second Coming on the Johnny Show, a comedy

My 44 Wives: A True Story of Multiple Personality

DMC—Dynamic Model of Consciousness

www.ingramcontent.com/pod-product-compliance
Lightning Source LLC
Chambersburg PA
CBHW022129280326
41933CB00007B/602